IMAGES OF
INDIA

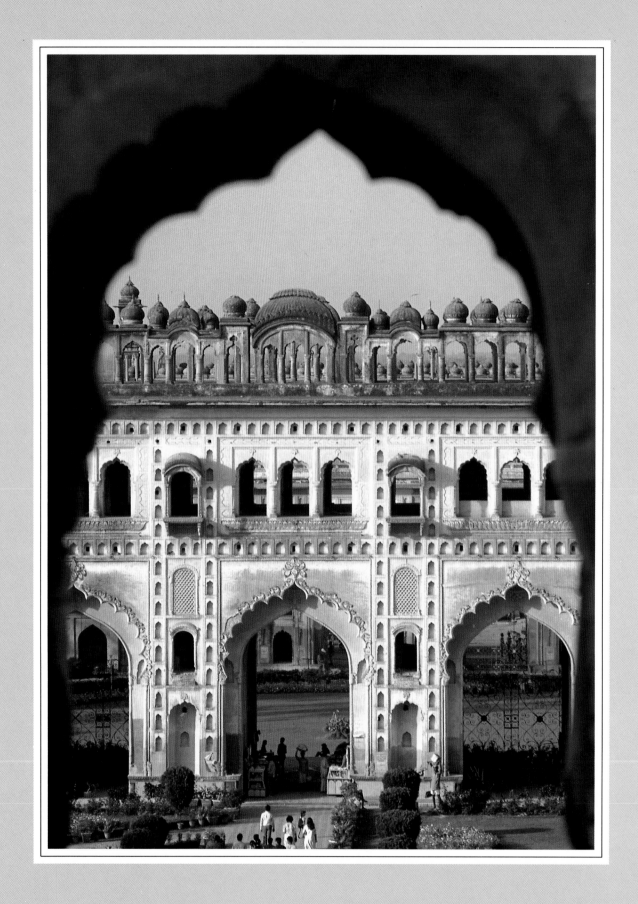

IMAGES OF
INDIA
SOPHIE BAKER

INTRODUCED BY
DERVLA MURPHY

PYRAMID BOOKS

Growing rice This plain in Kerala is a patchwork of paddy fields surrounded by coconut palms. Two men are taking refreshment while a woman is tending the rice crop.

First published in 1989
by Pyramid Books, an imprint of
The Hamlyn Publishing Group Limited
a division of The Octopus Publishing Group,
Michelin House, 81 Fulham Road, London SW3 6RB

ISBN 1-871-30782-1

Produced by Mandarin Offset
Printed and bound in Hong Kong

Introduction

In Britain, generations have grown up regarding India as not quite 'foreign'. After all, even those vast areas technically outside British India – Kashmir, Rajputana, Hyderabad, Mysore – were for many years manipulated by astute Political Agents. Also, there were oddly cosy connotations: wasn't Pandit Nehru a close personal friend of Lord Mountbatten? And, going back a bit, wasn't Queen Victoria devoted to her Indian Munshis? Then what about the Gurkhas? Tremendous chaps, absolutely fearless – won V.C.s all over the place! Contemporary Britain would have quite a different flavour had there never been a raj. No number of mere colonies, elsewhere, could have wrought such changes on the national consciousness.

To millions who have never been to India, the stereotypical raj became a reassuring part of their mental furniture. This imperial kaleidoscope depicted tigers, elephants, monkeys, snakes, jungles, ice-peaks, polo, riots, famines, spacious shady cantonment gardens, thronged pungent bazaars, creaking punkahs, unhygienic zenanas, devious lawyers, stupid babus, crafty Brahmin priests, romantically uniformed native regiments *(occasionally treacherous, usually gallant), deferential servants (some dependable, most shifty), shocking temples crowded with perversely lecherous gods and goddesses, ruthless zamindars, cowed peasants, emaciated coolies sleeping on pavements, obese maharajahs dwelling in gilded palaces, trigger-happy (but sporting) tribesmen on the Frontier, cunning money-lenders, pompously opulent durbars, sinister Hindu rites, bloody Muslim processions – the whole made to seem miraculously orderly and durable by the benign domination of the Viceroy and his supporting cast of dedicated, upright, stoical District Officers who always knew what was best for the natives.*

This kaleidoscope was accurate enough, as far as it went; thousands of personal and official records witness to its authenticity. Significantly, however, it omitted the most enduring Anglo-Indian achievement: that disinterested research into India's forgotten past done by such men as William Jones, James Pincep, Francis Buchanan, James Fergusson, James Tod, Alexander Cunningham. Inspired by passionate interest in the sub-continent's history and culture, these and many other unsubsidized enthusiasts revealed the antiquity and immense richness of Indian civilization to an astonished Europe – and a no less astonished India.

Then came Thomas Babington Macaulay's 1835 denunciation of Hindu culture – easily forgiven by the Indians, yet never forgotten. 'The Brahminical mythology' – Macaulay told the House of Commons – 'is so absurd that it necessarily debases every mind which receives it as truth ... All is hideous and grotesque and ignoble. As this superstition is of all superstitions the most irrational, and of all superstitions the most inelegant, so it is of all superstitions the most immoral.' Thereafter it was widely accepted that the Indians needed to be led – gently if possible, but very firmly – towards true civilization. To encourage them to study and respect their own past no longer seemed an appropriate task for English gentlemen. Thus the kaleidoscope edited out these scholars and represented India only as seen by chastely blinkered imperialists during the raj.

At that time the British were living through their most geographically expansive but mentally restricted epoch; while being singularly well-equipped to rule the sub-continent, they became increasingly ill-equipped even to try to understand it. This blunting of perception was inevitable, though it infuriated those scholars who were defiantly persisting with their researches. 'Natives' are much easier to govern if you can fervently believe in the superiority of your own culture.

The delectable irony is that the brief British raj – at once acquisitive and idealistic, destructive and creative – changed India, psychologically, less than it changed Britain. More than any other place on earth, 'the real India' was, is and almost certainly will remain impervious to alien influences. The majority of invaders stayed to be absorbed, gradually, over the centuries. The British soon went, bequeathing some valuable practical legacies. Calmly India assimilated what seemed useful and continued, inwardly, as before. Less complicated peoples are quickly degraded by unsuitable technology, mass tourism and seepage of trivialities from the West. India has eagerly accepted all these yet somehow the Indian Dharma survives. Hence the irresistible pull-back for those of us who belong to a frantically destabilized civilization that doesn't know where it's going and wouldn't know how to get there if it did.

New arrivals often find modern India repellent: corrupt, cynical, cruel, brash, greedy, and, to Western sensibilities, nauseatingly hypocritical. Trying to board an Indian bus, you would never imagine that you were in Gandhi-land, where comparatively recently non-violence was preached for decades. Listening to sleek businessmen and politicians at a fashionable New Delhi gathering, you would never suspect that the Congress Party fought for Independence so that India's poor need no longer be exploited.

Watching paunchy Brahmin priests fleecing lean peasants at a pilgrimage site, you would never suspect that asceticism is one of their ideals.

So what and where is this 'real India'? Anyway, isn't that phrase indefensibly limp and vague? We are after all considering a sub-continent – including every extremity of climate and terrain – where over 600 languages are spoken, where Tamils and people from the Punjab are more racially distinct than Portuguese and Swedes, where our European notion of the compact, coherent nation-state is meaningless. Yes, but ... Everyone who has explored this sub-continent knows that there is a 'real India', intuitively apprehensible though verbally indefinable. Where then is it to be found? Everywhere. And at any time. Although bound up with religion – or, more precisely, with spirituality – it doesn't necessarily manifest itself most obviously at solemn festivals or within the ambience of sacred places. It is robust, subtle, unsentimental, flexible – an intangible exciting emanation. We can gain from contacting it, but only if we don't pretend to understand, if we are humble enough to receive gratefully through our psychic pores what our grey cells can't handle.

India appalled me when I first cycled across the border, having spent a few months feeling at ease in Afghanistan and Pakistan. That was a grievous disappointment. For many years I had longed to experience India; it seemed a place to be 'experienced', rather than 'travelled through', because I had spent so long soaking myself in India-related books of every sort. And now what did I find? Prevaricating petty officials, persistent pilfering, everywhere too many people, deliberately maimed beggars, small children dying alone on city pavements... But why was I disillusioned? All this was part of my own Indian kaleidoscope. There had however been much more to it, which devastatingly eluded me on that first encounter.

Soon I fled, to spend six months in what was then the virtually Indian-free world of Dharamsala's Tibetan refugee camp. But, unlike the impregnably self-assured Victorian imperialists, I could not believe that revulsion from India was a mark of virtue; my negative response felt like a personal defeat. And so, before flying home, I cycled from Delhi to Nepal via Lucknow, Allahabad, Benares and Gorakhpur.

That was a strange journey, during which India claimed me. Much of the terrain was harsh, dusty, dull. Many of the villages were too starkly poor to seem romantically 'simple' and occasionally, in the most arid region, the villagers were too apathetic to be welcoming. But the majority, astonishingly, seemed able to find joy in their – to our eyes – bleakly impoverished existences. I remembered then a passage from Dr Radhakrishnan's essay on 'Ethics'. 'When the soul is at peace, the greatest sorrows are borne lightly. Life becomes more natural and confident. Changes in outer conditions do not disturb. We let our life flow of itself as the sea heaves or the flower blooms.' Somewhere between Lucknow and Allahabad I began to half-comprehend those words. Perhaps they were a realistic comment on Indian life, rather than the airy-fairy waffling of a well-heeled philosopher?

Benares prompted another tentative advance. There I realized that India is peculiarly tourist-proof, too fortified by its own baffling integrity to be vulnerable to those slings and arrows of outrageous vulgarity which elsewhere, since tourism became big business, have brutally killed 'the spirit of the place'.

In the terai of Nepal I avoided motor-tracks (not difficult) and so, while following a sandy path through golden elephant-grass, had the glorious good fortune to see a tiger. Sinuously he strolled across the path, scarcely ten yards ahead of me – either unaware of or (more likely) indifferent to my presence. That was a memorable day. A few hours later I was helped to ford a river by a courteous elephant evidently familiar with bicycles. Responding to a monosyllable from his mahout, he carefully picked mine up by the cross-bar, trunked it to his owner and then assisted me on to his back.

Next day, when my path expired in impenetrable jungle, I returned to India. In a small border town my camera was stolen from my dak-bungalow room by a son of the local policeman, who was also the chowkidar. Naively I hoped that a senior government official might help me to retrieve it; instead, he tried to attack me. But by then something so odd had happened that such contretemps felt unimportant. Although no more attracted to India than on arrival, the place had enthralled me.

A few years – and countries – later, I found myself walking into Bombay from the airport early one morning. In the surrounding shanty-town seethed the dispossessed; diseased pi-dogs nosed through decaying garbage; shrivelled cattle were being driven on to a desiccated grey-green wasteland where scores of men unself-consciously squatted with rusty tins of water to hand and often a hopeful pig in the background. Outside one sagging bamboo shack a graceful, dark-skinned young woman was washing her feet in water from a reeking pond with a lid of bright green scum. She looked up, and met my eyes, and smiled. That smile had a quality rarely found in our world. 'The real India' is often revealed in a smile.

During the following months, India was generous to me.

In Cochin, where the Kathakali troupe founded by Guru Paniker regularly dances, I was among an audience of three – normally an embarrassing situation, but these dancers don't care whether three or 3000 watch their performances. For them, being made-up is itself a solemn ritual taking two or three hours. Each face is painted all over: green for good characters, black for bad, red for villains, pink for women and saints. Their heavily jewelled brocade costumes are elaborate works of art, many four or five centuries old. Their language of gestures and expressions, based on the subtly eloquent use of eye, face, hand and foot muscles, has been so refined that over 800 words may be formed by using combinations of the twenty-four basic hand positions. They make no sound, apart from a few animal-like grunts emitted by the villain, and their slight, exquisitely stylized movements produce an effect of ineffable beauty. These Kathakali religious dances, based on the ancient puranas, are less an entertainment than a triumphant affirmation of the Immanence of the Divine, a journey into another sphere, an experience quintessentially Indian.

While settled in a remote Coorg village, I was invited to attend a neighbour's cremation. On my arrival in the forest glade, only two young men were watching the bonfire – lit from the hearth of the deceased, and from which her pyre would in turn be lit. Between the slender silver trunks of areca palms, indigo mountains bulked along the near horizon; above the green undergrowth glistened the dense burgundy-red leaves of incense-trees; against the cobalt sky two leafless, angular cotton-trees held aloft their blood-red, chalice-shaped blossoms.

Then, through the afternoon stillness, came the slow beat of distant drums and the plaintive wailing of Coorg horns. Far away, the little funeral procession was crossing pale gold stubble and purple-red plough-land – the mourners all clad in white.

The reverent, poignant ceremonials by the pyre took over an hour. Finally the husband moistened his dead wife's lips with water and everybody present touched her breast in a last gesture of grief and farewell. As the eldest son carried a burning brand from the bonfire, we women had to withdraw – a local custom. But at least one representative of each village family remained in the glade to ensure the body's reduction to ashes before sunset.

At dawn, the ashes were immersed in the sacred Cauvery river. Later, the site was lavishly watered and planted with paddy seeds; when these germinate, it is known that the departed spirit is at peace.

Elsewhere in Coorg I chanced upon a tiny stone temple (one or two thousand years old?) – looking no more than a large boulder, beneath the towering surrounding trees, with the few clumsy carvings on its facade almost erased by time. One could have walked by without noticing it but for a massive black Nandi facing the entrance. An elderly priest – tall, stooped, very thin – tended the shrine; daily he did puja, a ceremony rarely attended by anyone. (The Coorgis are not great temple-goers.)

Early one morning, before the sun had lifted the night mist, I walked to this tranquil spot between the scarlet cascades of high poinsettia hedges. The Brahmin had not yet arrived. Nandi and I were alone in the shade of giant nellige, peepul, jack-fruit, mango and palm trees. The sky was a cool fresh blue, emerald-streaked by parakeets, and only isolated bird-calls broke the silence. Never have I forgotten the peace of that place.

The Brahmin, being a devout man of the gods, ignored me. In a stone hut near the temple he roused the sacrificial fire, then took his brass pitcher to the well near Nandi. From the open door I watched those holy flames jumping and lengthening in the gloom: awesome links with the Garhapatya fires of the first Aryans in India. When the Brahmin took his laden tray to the temple I stood a few yards from him, at the foot of the half-dozen deeply worn stone steps leading up to the shrine. Intoning prayers, he sat cross-legged before the four-armed Shiva, dancing on the body of the demon of delusion, and Ganesh – Shiva's endearingly elephant-headed, pot-bellied son by his consort Parvati, the mountain goddess. The sun grew hot as I watched him making his oblations, ringing his bell, wafting incense, presenting garlands, repeatedly cupping his hands over the sacred flame of the dish-lamp. Occasionally, in India, the power of tradition obliterates time: a sensation both disturbing and releasing. So it was in that crude temple, as the Brahmin performed rituals that already were old when Christ was born.

And then there was Cape Comorin ... Suddenly one sees the sea – or rather, three seas – and a temple on a rock about half-a-mile off-shore. And that's it. Cape Comorin is emphatically final, a promontory unmistakably farther south than the rest of the sub-continent. Steps lead down to the turbulent confluence of the Gulf of Mannar, the Indian Ocean and the Arabian Sea. In these revered waters pilgrims 'take bath' and do puja, creating that incomparable atmosphere of devout gaiety which marks so many of Hinduism's less accessible holy places.

Neck-deep in swirling foam, I remembered that other frontier of rock and eternal snow – the long base of the Indian triangle, 2000 miles away, with 1,138,814 square miles and hundreds of millions of people in between. And I marvelled at the durability, elusiveness and strange beauty of that mix of rank superstition and sophisticated metaphysics which unites the fair-skinned shepherds of the high Himalayan valleys and the dark-skinned fishermen of the Coromandel Coast.

Dervla Murphy

Bombay

As the commercial capital, this is the most cosmopolitan of all Indian cities. Built on an island linked by bridges to the neighbouring state of Maharashtra, it is a busy and thriving port. Where castes and creeds intermingle, Bombay has become a destination for large numbers of village folk who arrive there every day from all over the country. They come with a dream in their hearts, aspiring to bring about change from the persistent grind of the wheel of struggle to survive– a sentiment that pervades the lives of the majority of the population of the world's largest democracy.

Shanty town dwellers, Bombay A Bustee (slum) family of six inhabit this wood and cardboard construction in a shanty town near the centre of the city. The interior measures barely two metres square. The owner has decorated the exterior of his home with potted plants and posters advertising thriller movies.

Gymkhana Club, Bombay The British left India in 1947, but institutions such as this club have been preserved. Now it is patronized by Bombay's social elite.

Overleaf A young woman walks alone along Chowpatty beach, the tail of her chiffon sari fluttering in a gentle sea breeze. The sun sets behind the high-rise blocks of Malabar Hill, a leafy enclave where Bombay's film stars have their homes.

Coastal region of Kerala

This lush strip of mountainous tropical land in the south west is blessed with rich and fertile soil producing tea, coffee, bananas, mangoes, pineapples and other exotic fruits. Many spices including cardamom, pepper and eucalyptus are also grown here. There are thousands of hectares of rubber plantations and thick groves of coconut palms.

As abundant as it is in produce, so it is the most densely populated of all India's states and the one with the highest ratio of protestants and catholics. Christianity was firmly established by the Portuguese who developed a prosperous port in the city of Cochin over 500 years ago.

In recent years the people of Kerala, the Malayalis, have been more progressive and politically aware than those elsewhere. Sixty per cent of them are literate, twice the national average. As one travels on the highways and through the small villages, schoolchildren in their crisply starched uniforms, young boys and girls with fresh flowers in their hair, huge piles of schoolbooks in their arms, are a common sight.

Fishermen of Kerala Behind the long
sandy coastline of Kerala there are chains
of freshwater lagoons, connected by an
intricate network of waterways. Seagulls
hover above the boats, hopeful of
snatching a fishy morsel from the
morning's catch.

Left A fisherman repairs his boat, known
as a wallam, which is similar in style to the
Chinese sampan.

Harvesting coconuts, Kerala The fruit is split in half and left in the sun until the dried flesh can easily be separated from the shell. Oil is extracted from the flesh and the fibre from the shell is used for matting and heavy-duty ropes.

The barter system A Malayali peasant, who is given bananas instead of wages, carries his barter five kilometres to the nearest market so that he can raise some money to purchase other goods.

Tea plantations Monsoon clouds gather over the hills of the Western Ghats. The humidity of the monsoon season – from June to October – provides ideal conditions for tea plantations. As with many other crops, women form an important part of the labour force during harvest. This woman has knotted a piece of sacking round her waist to make a pouch for the tea leaves.

Construction workers Malayali women earn ten rupees a day (less than 50 pence) on a brick construction site. Despite the rigours of working ten hours with only one short break, carrying heavy loads on their heads, they create a cheerful image in their patterned skirts and brightly coloured blouses.

With their picks raised high above their heads, these men appear to be performing a ritual dance as they carry out repairs on a main trunk road. Shallow round baskets are used to move the caked earth.

Village market, Kerala Being more durable and lighter to carry than those made of clay, plastic buckets and bowls are becoming more popular with the villagers. Assorted cooking utensils are suspended from the roof in string bags. Pieces of cardboard have been used to create a little shade for the piles of fruit.

Riches of Kerala The ivory and spices found in the region have long attracted traders from both east and west. Some believe King Solomon's ships anchored there around 1000 BC; the Romans and Greeks stocked up their galleys with rare commodities, and the earliest Christian settlers arrived from Syria. Islam was introduced by Arab traders who stopped in Kerala en route for the Far East.

Today the elephant is still a magnificent beast of burden, its trunk curled round a load of coconut palms as it makes its stately progress along a village street.

Impervious to his rather bizarre appearance, this man is using an umbrella as a sunshade.

A backwater in Kerala Coconut palms are reflected in the water, providing a tranquil vantage point for a pair of mynah birds. These exotic birds enjoy a very different habitat from other members of the starling family who are often seen in the centre of London.

River transport Canopies of palm fronds
lean out from the banks to give some
shade to the bamboo-covered boats. These
serve as both taxis and freight carriers. The
surface of the water is studded with water-
lilies, which sway in the wash of the boats.

Above At Alleppy near the coast, a young
boy darts through a bevy of hand-reared
ducks, crowded round a shallow pond.

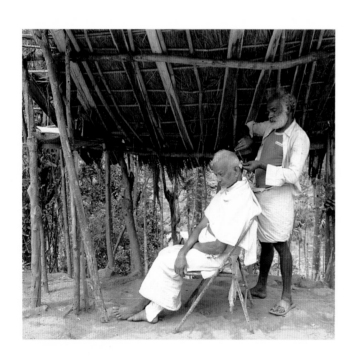

An elephant's day Every working elephant has his own keeper, a *mahout*, who is invariably his trainer too. They are usually together for the whole of the elephant's working life. Their day starts at 5am when the beast is bathed in the nearest river, where he is submerged and scrubbed with a piece of jackfruit skin. After a breakfast of gruel or rice the pair set off for work, maybe some kilometres away. The pace is a steady six kilometres per hour. Allowing for one hour's meal break in the middle of the morning, they work for no more than ten hours. After a dinner of bananas and sugar cane, the elephant will be let loose in the jungle to roam freely during the night, wearing a brass bell around his neck so that his keeper can find him the following day.

Left A gentlemen's hair-dressing salon.

Above Mahabalipuram, south of the state capital of Madras, is a small sea port of some 6000 people. Lobster, prawns and small sharks are the fishermen's main catch. The town is famous for its cave temples, full of magnificent and elaborate stone carvings, and the enchanting shore temple seen here in the background, a monument dedicated to the Hindu God, Shiva.

Right Large cut-out cardboard images of south Indian movie stars dominate this street corner in Madurai. The Indian film industry is the largest in the world and every big city has its own movie studios.

Tamil Nadu

*D*ue east of Kerala lies the state of Tamil Nadu. Divided by the mountain range of the Western Ghats, it has a very different geographical character. Much of the landscape is flat and sparse and despite the occasional relief of mango groves and tall coconut trees, the Tamils have to till hard in this coastal region to cultivate their paddy, orchards of cashews and peanuts, watermelons, ragi – a kind of mustard seed – and salt fields set beside backwaters that are filled by the monthly high tides.

Tamil women Every morning, after cleaning inside and around the home, the householder will use coloured chalks or powdered rice to create *rangoli* patterns at the doorstep. These are an invitation to the gods to visit the home.

During the long dry season, drinking water is always scarce and the communal well is always crowded. These women have to crouch awkwardly in the cramped space, fearful of spilling a drop of the precious liquid.

Harvest festival The celebration of Sankranti, the harvest festival, is one of the most popular events in Tamil Nadu. On the second day, the cows and bullocks have their horns painted in bright colours and are covered in decorations, before taking part in a thanksgiving ceremony with all the children of the neighbourhood.

Left With their saris lifted above the muddy water, women are bent over the paddy-field planting rice.

There is no national health service in India in the form enjoyed in Europe, although the large cities are fairly well served by government hospitals. However, as two-thirds of the population live in the countryside, many of them in remote regions, the people are dependent on a small number of primary health centres and various medical missions financed from overseas.

Most people still favour prayer to the gods or a consultation with their local self-appointed ayurvedic practitioners who prescribe native remedies. They maintain that their forefathers were well enough served in this way. It is extremely difficult for a doctor to care for the poorer rural communities as he or she will find it virtually impossible to receive any form of financial backing, but there are a few who are willing to devote their medical skills to such work, with only the satisfaction of knowing that they are providing their patients with a rare but much needed service.

Dr Gladys Indira, a devout catholic, has set up a small surgery near Chingleput, 40 kilometres south of Madras, where she treats some 8000 people who live in the small town and in the surrounding villages.

Her doctor father also worked in the remote villages of Tamil Nadu at a time

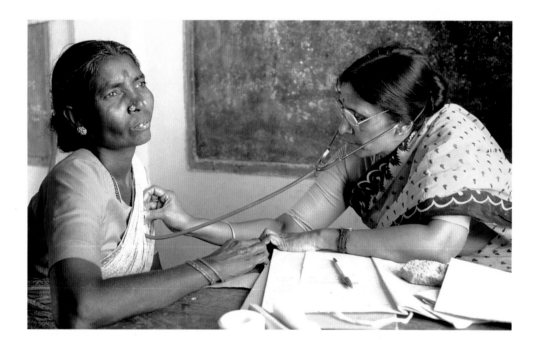

when there was no electricity or transport. Through his example she nurtured an ambition to enter the medical profession and work for the poorer communities. His death strengthened her resolve and she chose this location because there was no other doctor resident there at the time, not even to administer elementary first aid.

Dr Gladys holds two clinics daily of three hours each, when she gives injections and tablets, and dresses wounds. She makes local visits in between. The most common ailments are typhoid, TB, dysentry, hepatitis, scabies and venereal diseases. Due to the lack of preventative vaccines there are many cases of diphtheria, tetanus and poliomyelitis, as well as various diseases resulting from undernourishment. She does not charge a consultation fee but makes the patients contribute towards the cost of drugs. She derives her income from treating the tourists who come from all over the world to visit the local temples.

For Dr Gladys, healing is a divine job. 'I pray to God to give me a simple heart to live among these people and make myself one among them.'

Mahabalipuram Young girls on the seashore wait for the sun to rise.

Mahabalipuram Many stonemasons, called
acharis, are seen throughout the back
streets. From dawn to sunset the noise of
granite being cut and chiselled fills the air.

Hinduism

I ndia has a population of around 800 million at present but this figure is increasing by 15 million each year. Eighty per cent of the people practise the Hindu faith. Around 1500 BC the Vedic scriptures were written and from these evolved some of the ideologies of Hinduism. Its followers believe that they will all go through a series of rebirths until eventually spiritual salvation is attained and they are freed from the cycle.

Hinduism is primarily concerned with the nature of the universe and the relationship between man and the divine. One omnipotent God is recognized as one universal soul, but each individual chooses from amongst the hundreds of gods, representatives and incarnations of many different forces, some shown in the pictures laid out on the pavement (left), which they would like to deify and worship.

Above This small boy leaves the temple perched on his father's shoulder. His head has just been shaved and his hair offered in thanks to Vishnu, the family god.

Forms of worship Hindus feel free to choose for themselves in which form they wish to worship their family deity. Each god is associated with an animal, their conveyor. In India, auspiciousness is not just contained with the temple walls. The gods are invoked everywhere – floors of houses, doorsteps, even on the pavements – exquisite drawings in coloured chalks containing a religious message within the intricate lines.

Under the umbrella of the omnipresent god there are three main physical representations: Brahma, the creator, Vishnu, the preserver and Shiva, the destroyer of evil.

Left Outside a temple dedicated to Shiva, a young girl sells garlands of marigolds and coconuts, the traditional food of the gods.

Meenakshi temple, Madurai The cloisters
of the temple provide welcome shade.
Two thousand years ago this city was the
capital of the Pandya kings and a
renowned centre of Tamil culture.

Acts of worship The Hindu philosophy
preaches two totally contradictory states of
mind: Dharma, one's intentional actions,
and Kharma, one's fate, that which is
preordained. Yet worshippers believe that
Kharma is a direct result of one's Dharma.
One of the most important practices of the
faith is Puja, the act of prayer. Here,
villagers join together in Puja at a festival
to celebrate the birth of Lord Krishna.

Above The temple elephant is trained to
give thanks and a blessing to those who
come to worship.

Kalakshetra, school of dance

I ndian dance is a means of understanding life. Its intention is to enhance the better part of human nature and all that which is beautiful and to pass it on to future generations.

For over 2000 years, Bharatanatyan dance has re-enacted stories of love and hope, tales of the gods and demons. It is a body language of classical dance.

Kalakshetra, the school where Bharatanatyan is studied, was founded near Madras in 1936 by Rukmini Devi, a young Brahmin girl who broke with tradition and married an Irishman some thirty years her senior. In her, the dance found a protectress. She revived the tradition, and explored new forms while retaining the purity and classicism. Without her intervention the form would have died.

Dance training takes six years. For all the students, studies in Sanskrit, Tamil, yoga and painting are also compulsory. The day starts at 5am with prayer. They worship under the shade of an enormous Banyan tree. Although the students come from different denominations, they are taught that religion is united on a mountain top where Almighty God sits. Everyone approaches him via a different route.

Final-year students perform in a large auditorium dedicated to Shiva, the God of dance. The dancers are known as the brides of God – it is thought that Shiva has the world as his body and all the existing sounds of the universe are his vocal expressions. The moon and the stars are his ornaments. Every morning the students pray to this cosmic consciousness which pervades the universe.

Dance drama is based on the Hindu epics and simple folk legends. The aim is to uplift and inspire the audience. There should be a communication between them and the artist – a shared experience. A large vocabulary of expressions has to be learned. The movements of the eyes, arms, hands, feet and face are synchronized to music to relate a story. Great skill is required to express a range of deep emotions from compassion and love to self-abandonment. Each gesture is a response of admiration and ecstasy.

The intention of Bharatanatyan dance is to open up man's or woman's inner nature, their spiritual psyche. It is this art form that is considered a refining force for the self-improvement of man.

Music studies at Kalakshetra These include South Indian vocal music, the veena (stringed instrument with dragon and big bell), flute, mridangam (percussion) and the violin.

As little of the music is recorded in written form, students have to learn by copying their own guru. The study therefore requires intense concentration and an ability to memorize quickly whatever the tutor plays.

Priority is given to the mastery of an art accompanied by a world of knowledge. In a world of fast-changing values, Kalakshetra is an oasis of purity.

Temple dancers Prior to the founding of
Kalakshetra, dancing was confined to the
temples, relating only religious themes.
The girls who danced during the day were
prostitutes by night. The population had
been losing touch with this part of their
heritage. These dancers are taking part in
an ancient romance movie that is being
made in the Meenakshi temple in Madurai.
This section of the temple is crowded with
gopurams, supported by pillars decorated
with stucco figures of gods, goddesses and
mythical animals.

Kathakali This is performed in Kerala. Its origins also go back 2000 years but the dance form seen today is about 300 years old. The word means 'story – play' and, like Bharatanatyan, legends and parables are told through various combinations and movements of the eyes, hands and feet.

Performances can last all through the night preceded by three hours spent applying the elaborate make-up. The exquisite beauty of the choreography is magical and the dedication of the dance troupe, awesome.

O f the 20 per cent of Indians who do not practise Hinduism, 14 per cent are Muslim, three per cent are Sikhs and the remaining three per cent are Jains, Parsees, Buddhists and Christians. The 80 per cent majority who are Hindus live in the villages where society is firmly based on the caste system.

This is an order of life that evolved in the Vedic Age around 1500 BC as Hinduism emerged, in which the Brahmins, originally heads of the family, and now spiritual leaders, priests and teachers, came at the top of the pecking order. Next in line came the Kshatryas, the warriors and protectors, then the Vaysyas, the merchants, and at the bottom came the Sudra, those who served the upper castes as clothes washers, household servants, agricultural labourers, craftsmen and the like. Then there were those outside the system altogether, the Untouchables, renamed Harijans – Children of God – by the Mahatma Gandhi.

Household duties Two women prepare chappatis and vegetable cutlets for the evening meal in the courtyard of their home in Patna in the state of Bihar. Another women is deftly slicing limes to make pickle. The young dhobi (washerwoman) girl in Andhra Pradesh practises the traditional method of washing clothes.

Village India

The massive landmass of India consists of vast sand deserts, splendid mountain ranges, dense rain forests and kilometre upon kilometre of endless plains. The majority of the population lives in the villages of India. They constitute the soul and the backbone of Indian society, with livelihoods depending on an agricultural economy.

Veeravally (photographed here), a village in Andhra Pradesh, has a population of about 2000, comprised of farmers, shepherds, a goldsmith, weavers, potters, store-keepers, dhobis, basket makers, tailors, carpenters, blacksmiths, barbers, and two communities of Harijans living outside the village boundary. These are the Mala, scheduled casted who traditionally deal with all forms of dead flesh, and the Madiga, those who labour on the land.

Outside the caste system The village cobbler (left), a Harijan, lives on the outskirts of this village in Andhra Pradesh. Any task involving the flesh of a dead animal is undertaken by a Harijan. Apart from leatherwork and shoemaking, Harijans beat the drum at all village functions, including weddings and funerals.

Village celebrations These young boys
are washing a goat shortly before its head
is to be chopped off as part of the
celebrations to mark Divali, festival of
lights and the Hindu New Year. The
festivities will include a feast of kid and
specially prepared sweets.

Above A villager gives himself a morning
shower at the communal well by tipping a
bucket of water over his head.

Agricultural workers For a daily wage of a few rupees, these men will work for up to ten hours. Here they are beating *jower* – a millet from which flour is prepared – to separate the grain from the stalks.

Left The monsoon rains are welcomed by these villagers in Bihar, a state which often suffers from prolonged drought.

Tie-and-dye weaving

With the introduction of powerlooms a large proportion of the textile industry in India is mechanized today. Weavers are the second largest trained workforce in the country, there being over ten million labouring in city-based mills. Fortunately, in many villages in the vicinity of Hyderabad, the capital city of Andhra Pradesh, handloom weaving continues to flourish as there still is a market prepared to pay a high price for quality silk saris rather than less for quantity.

For the Reddy family, shown here, tie-and-dye weaving is a way of life. Known as Ikat, the design is one of the most attractive and popular but also one of the most complicated to produce. The ladies of the household commence the process, boiling and spinning the silk before deftly threading it, strand upon strand, on to a fan-shaped shank, and tying strips of rubber according to the design, on to the yarn.

Each set of yarn has to be very tightly wrapped to prevent the colour from seeping through when the silk is dipped into the various dyes. Vats are filled with watered hues and the silk dyed in different colours – dramatically contrasting combinations of deep pink, bright green and white with gold thread, bottle green, brown and white, purple, scarlet, vermillion, jade green, plum mauve and other lovely colours.

A family business The rubber bindings are carefully removed when the yarn has dried and it is stretched once again on to the winding frame, where the impression of the design begins to emerge. It is then transferred on to wooden bobbins and placed in shuttles ready for weaving the silken lengths.

Only the Reddy brothers work on the looms which were constructed by their grandfather over 50 years ago. For up to six hours a day they stand inside a large trough dug into the floor, a much more comfortable position than sitting cross-legged in the traditional style.

There are 5000 threads in the width of each sari and nearly 15,000 in its length. Between them, the family can produce about fifteen garments every month which ensures them sufficient income to buy food and clothing, and enough seed and fertilizer to cultivate the four hectares they own on the periphery of their village.

A length of Ikat The family work as an efficient team, toiling together slowly and silently. The complicated art of adjusting the rubber strips to lay out the design, with its many motifs including the shape of an elephant, demands skill, but as the children grow up playing around the looms and watching their parents work, they learn the craft as they mature. It is the constant dividing, counting of thread, tying and dyeing that creates a length of Ikat.

*I*n most villages clay-firing is usually undertaken every other week. For two days the pots are submerged in hot ashes of smouldering straw in a large trench.

Potters belong to the Sudra caste. Their contribution to the village community is vital. Apart from making water pots, they also supply roof tiles, bricks for house construction and waist-high vats in which families can store their grain safely out of the reach of rats and mice.

The potter's wheel Water pots are made by the traditional method with no mechanical aids to spin the wheel. Skilfully bending his fingers, the potter shapes the wet clay into the characteristic ridges.

Overleaf Although photographed in Andhra Pradesh, these gypsy women have their roots in the western desert state of Rajasthan. Due to the endemic water shortage they travel throughout the country with their families and are often found working on building sites in the larger cities and in constructing the country's rural highways. Tradition dictates that they carry their entire wealth in the form of silver trinkets, stitched to their head-dresses, and ivory bangles, worn the length of their arms.

Child labour

Concern is continually expressed in the Indian press over the exploitation of small children working in factories. Children constitute six per cent of the labour force in India. They are usually called apprentices although many of them do extremely strenuous work. Through sheer economic necessity, many children are exploited by their families, usually to help with agricultural work.

In Tamil Nadu, there is an established tradition of employing children in the hand-made matchbox industry that goes back fifty years. It has always been a big boon to the economically backward Tamils, living in one of the country's most drought-prone areas, to have extra work that can be done in the home. Every member of the family could lend a hand making the boxes and every little extra hand meant a little extra money.

As more small industries developed, so the practice of hauling children to the factories began. When the government lifted the production ceiling on hand-made matchbox units, child employment grew phenomenally.

Some of the recruits are barely of kindergarten age and employers are willing to transport children from villages over 40 kilometres from their homes. As the buses do more than one trip, some children are collected at 3am and left

by the drivers half-asleep outside the factories long before dawn breaks, so that a full work force is ready to start the day when the gates are opened at 6am.

An estimated 40,000 children are working in the match factories of the small town of Sivakasi alone. More than half the workers are girls and they squat on the floor in rows, filling frames with flints. They are paid for each bracket they fill, each with 2500 flints, sufficient for 50 boxes of matches. The older girls and young women fill and label the boxes, working in overcrowded sheds. Young men dip the filled frames into the sulphur and impose a strict code of discipline on the youngsters.

Village school, Veeravally Although only about a hundred people living in this village can read and write proficiently, many of the children attend the local school where the daughter of the village postman teaches. Five subjects are taught – reading, writing, healthcare, mathematics and some social science. An attendance fee of two rupees daily (about ten pence) is charged but the teacher will waive this if a child's parents cannot afford to pay. All the children sit together, ignoring each other's caste.

Above Television is now a potent force throughout India. Here, in Tamil Nadu, the children watch the Sunday afternoon movie on a set placed in the shade of a large neem tree.

Students at Santi Niketan Literary Nobel
Prize winner, Rabindranath Tagore was
born in Bengal in 1861. He grew up in a
cultured ambiance, his family including
musicians, artists and social reformers. He
possessed exceptional artistic talents and
was renowned not just as a prolific writer
of poetry, novels, short stories, sermons,
journalistic essays and dramatic works but
also as a musician and a painter.

In 1901 he founded a school and
university at Santi Niketan, photographed
here. His vision was for students to acquire
knowledge through an understanding of
man's relation with nature and a
knowledge of their cultural heritage rather
than by the conventional methods
preferred by the British Raj.

Lucknow, Uttar Pradesh A tailor sits
outside a friend's store which only sells tin
trunks, but in many shapes and sizes.

Lucknow, Uttar Pradesh

From the late 18th century, Lucknow emerged as a capital Muslim city through the rule of the Nawabs of Oudh. As a family they were primarily concerned with music, dance and stylish courtly living. For nearly a hundred years, extravagance and elegance were the order of the day and there was an atmosphere of friendly tolerance between the princely family and the governing British.

However, in 1857, mutiny erupted within the ranks of Indian soldiers enlisted by the imperial colonels. The Residency of the governor was the scene of some of the most extraordinary feats of heroism and courage, and it was there that the century-long struggle for independence from the British took root. Lucknow is still a predominantly Muslim city with a rich heritage of Islamic culture, exotic cuisine and lovingly constructed monuments.

Forms of transport A brand-new cycle rickshaw is imaginatively decorated with plastic buttons, brightly coloured plastic and a photograph of the owner's favourite film actress. The traditional taxi service of horse and cart contrasts with the modern poster on a billboard advertising a store where denim jeans, teeshirts and trainers can be purchased.

Food marketing Indian cooking is much enjoyed throughout the world, due in part to its great variety of produce. Fresh fruit and vegetables grow in abundance but the tropical temperatures create problems for retailing and storage – hence the popularity of rice, lentils and pulses, as part of the daily staple diet. Here, the well stocked trader also offers ready-to-eat snacks, spiced wheat products and sweet biscuits, all of which have a long shelf life.

Above The nuts and dried fruit displayed in sparkling glass jars include almonds, cashews, pistachios, walnuts, raisins, figs and apricots.

The Imambara A view across the Gomti river, tributary of the Ganges, from the Imambara, the glorious tomb built for himself by the Nawab Asuf-ud-Daula before his death in 1797.

Calcutta

Once the imperial capital of India, before the British moved their government headquarters to New Delhi, Calcutta represents the worst and yet the best of India. The blame for the visions of disease, squalor, poverty and death are in part due to the problem created by the 1947 Partition Laws. East Bengal was annexed as a part of Pakistan, a new country for the Muslims, causing a massive influx of Hindu refugees fleeing from their homeland.

The climate also adds to the problem as people living in Bihar, Orissa and Bengal – states which are prone to the worst of famine and floods – arrive daily in vast numbers, hoping to find work.

Yet Calcutta is a city with great soul. Students, film-makers, sculptors, journalists, artisans, painters, poets and actors create an atmosphere in which they all thrive. They are deeply proud of their Bengali heritage and vow that there is no place on earth where they would rather make their home. Despite its crumbling edifices Calcutta is a city of great beauty with wide tree-lined avenues, mansions and apartment buildings of noble proportions, and the Maidan, the large and beautiful park in the city centre.

Above In the hope of receiving a few rupees, this young man has buried his head in a hole in the pavement in order to attract the attention of passers by.

Right Across the river from Howrah station, *bustee* (slum) dewllers take their morning bath on the banks of the Hooghly.

Overleaf Pavement dwellers in a Muslim neighbourhood of Calcutta start their day.

Right This armless child, a begging bowl at his side, sleeps in the midday sun on the pavement of Chowringee, Calcutta's busiest thoroughfare. Such sights are pathetically commonplace and invariably invoke sentiments of sadness and horror in the hearts of travellers to the city.

No other city in India suffers the monotonous regularity of power cuts and breakdowns in the telephone system in quite the same way as Calcutta does. When the monsoon rains commence, the inadequate drainage system becomes blocked and the waters rise, instantly turning the streets into fast-moving canals and forcing the ever congested traffic to a complete halt.

Street scenes such as this one are commonplace. One firm is contracted to repair a burst water main, another to reconstruct the roadway. In the meantime there is a strike amongst some of the labourers and technicians and possibly, because of funds being diverted, also a failure to fulfil the contract.

West Bengal has a Marxist government at odds within a country ruled by Congress – hence political confusion and disarray within the unions. However, most people living in Calcutta have adopted an attitude of tolerance to the chronic disorder which governs their lives.

Indian Railways

A legacy from the British Raj, the Indian Railways system is the fourth largest in the world. Surprisingly too, although it is not a speedy system, it has a very high standard of time-keeping and reliability.

Apart from the inevitable congestion of travelling in and out of the large cities during rush hours, a rail journey can be a very pleasurable experience. A little forethought and planning is always advisable and for longer trips, booking in advance is necessary.

Every air-conditioned sleeping compartment has its own attendant who will supply blankets and freshly laundered bedclothes. Orders are taken for meals and a variety of curries are served, both vegetarian and non-vegetarian. One can book a morning call and be awakened with a flask of hot tea or coffee.

Every main-line terminus throbs with activity, as hawkers of every description ply their goods. There are people selling fruit, nuts, sweets, clay cups of sweet tea, all kinds of reading matter, children's toys, brightly coloured plastic bangles and much more. There are also sacred cows who are left to roam on their own.

Left Bengali peasants en route for Calcutta transporting boxes of fresh mangoes to sell in the city market.

Right At Bombay's Victoria Terminus passengers sleep on sacks in the departure hall waiting for the train that will take them back to their village. Few of Bombay's domestic servants and hotel workers were born in the city. They mostly come from villages in neighbouring states and once a year they return home to spend some time with their families.

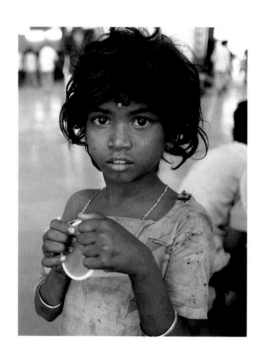

Itinerant children Sleeping and living in a railway terminus is a way of life for some children. This young boy, with his begging bowl, barely remembers the village where he grew up, so accustomed is he now to a hand-to-mouth existence, dependent on the goodwill of others.

A Sadhu on the banks of the Ganges at Allahabad – a Hindu pilgrim who feels he has completed his usefulness in active life and has chosen to end his days alone, wandering in search of spiritual peace and contemplation.

The Ganges

The river runs from its source in the Himalayan mountains 2400 kilometres to the Bay of Bengal. Its greatness is attributed to the sanctity accorded to its waters by the Hindus. To the devout, immersion in the river will absolve them of guilt.

Every Hindu would like to be cremated on its bank, or failing that, to have their ashes cast into it. Sons will travel thousands of kilometres from all over the country especially to deposit their father's and mother's remains in the murky waters.

Despite the presence of rotting corpses and city effluence, the Ganges is regarded as pure and spiritually cleansing. Thousands of poems and hymns have been composed eulogising its sanctity and to chant these in sight of its shores will atone for all the sins of one's previous lives and clear the way for rebirth in the highest form.

Benares, India's most religious city, is situated on the banks of the Ganges. Further upstream are Allahabad and Hardwar, holy cities where the Kumbh Mela is celebrated – a religious fete of massive proportions where many thousands of pilgrims immerse themselves simultaneously into the holy waters.

Rajasthan

T*he dry scrub, pebbled rocks and drifting sands of the Thar Desert of Rajasthan create an illusion of inhospitality. But within this rugged and sunbaked landscape are enchanting small villages, clustered under edifices of magnificent crumbling forts and stone palaces.*

Rajasthan is a state of great beauty and legend. It is the land of princely Rajput families, Kshatrya warriors descended from the Greek soldiers of the Kushan Empire who founded small princedoms with their own small armies of protectors. In time, the Brahmins absorbed them into their own communities as their defenders.

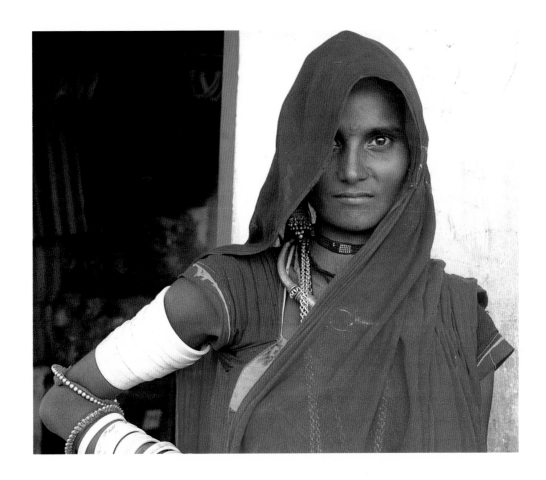

Rajput women As soon as a girl is physically mature she is expected to keep her face covered at all times in male company and in front of strangers. The reason for this requirement is that a peaceful and harmonious life will only be achieved through respect. When people become too open, it is believed that they lose regard for each other.

Overleaf Year in, year out the monsoon rains have failed to reach Udaipur District but when they come, the soil responds speedily to the moisture and the sandy desert is miraculously transformed into a fertile green meadow.

The walls of this typical Rajasthani house in the western desert state bordering Pakistan have been plastered with a mixture of mud, cowdung and chopped straw. They are decorated with folk art showing a naive imagination in honour of Dashera, an important Hindu festival which celebrates the triumph of good over evil.

Making curd from goats' milk All the milk products are stored in a large metal cage in a shaded corner of the kitchen, safe from cats and rats. Every meal in the household is accompanied with delicious raita, a mixture of the curd, onion, chilli, salt and turmeric. Elaborate preparations for a special feast will include tomato curry, garlic pickle, ladies' fingers, onions soaked in fresh lime juice, ghee ladled on to chappattis made from black millet, all washed down with a beaker full of fresh lassi made from the curd which has cooled in a large earthenware pot.

A Rajput farmer Unable to disguise his
pleasure at the arrival of the monsoon rain
after an absence of four years, this Rajput
farmer joyfully pulls the weeds from his
crop of maize.

Form of dress Few women in Rajasthan
dress in the traditional sari favoured in the
rest of the country. Instead they wear a
simple calf-length skirt with a short-sleeved
blouse. They then twine a cotton shawl,
printed in traditional floral pattern, around
their waists and shoulders and over their
heads. Here they are washing clothes at
the well, the focal point of their lives.

Above A familiar sight on the highways
near Udaipur: barefoot women walking in
unison, baskets filled to the brim with the
cow dung cakes used as cooking fuel,
balanced on their heads.

Cattle farming Cows play an important role in the economy of Rajasthan. A cattle farmer living in the desert will rise at 4am to lead his herd to a distant oasis, sometimes as far as ten kilometres. But four successive years of drought in the state created an unprecedented crisis and a struggle to preserve the dying beasts began.

Camps funded by the state were set up around the small towns to look after cattle forced to migrate. Sadly for most, help came too late. Thousands of Rajput farmers lost their animals and their livelihoods, and now many are faced with the lengthy uphill task of rebuilding their herds.

कृपयाधीरेचलिये

Quarry workers Men and women take a rest from working in a quarry near Chittor. The ladies are sitting in the shade of a disused centopath, a holy shrine abandoned by its Brahmin owner who formerly farmed the land.

Above The camel is a familiar sight in Rajasthan. Its ability to drink and store enough water for three days, makes it an ideal beast of burden in the desert.

Bhil tribals near Jodhpur Similar to the Rajputs in character, their main qualities are those of pride and honour. Surroundings and material wealth are of little value, their motto being – 'What is in your blood is what matters. Strong blood makes you walk tall.'

Unlike other castes and tribals they consider sharing a hookah of opium or tobacco with another as a sign of brotherhood and friendship.

133

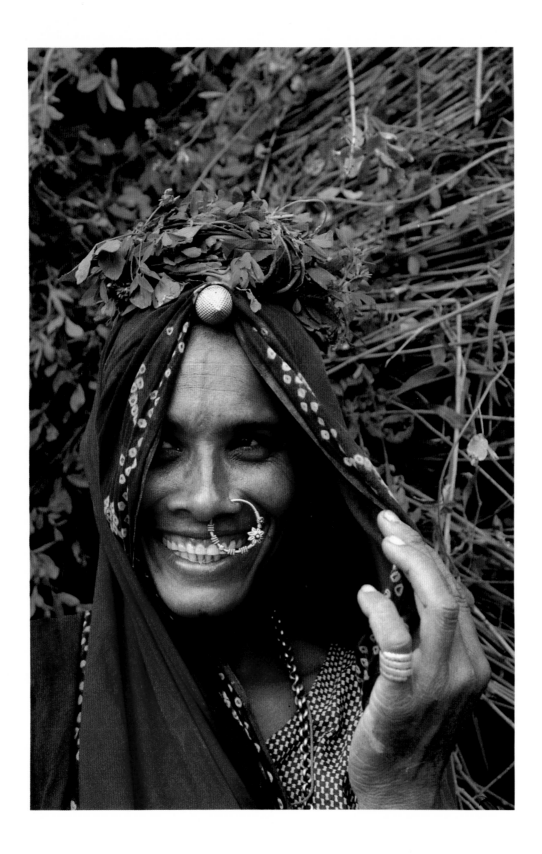

Delhi

The capital of India is a glorious city, with wide tree-lined avenues and spacious colonial-style bungalows set in immaculate gardens and extensive well-watered lawns. Visitors are overwhelmed by the majesty of the Parliament buildings, built of pale pink stone imported from neighbouring Rajasthan and designed by Britain's foremost turn-of-the-century architect, Sir Edwin Lutyens.

New Delhi was developed by the British both as the new seat of parliament and to station their troops in a more central position than Calcutta in the east. As the old city had always been an overcrowded and congested place, the land chosen was to the south, a flat plain interspersed with gardens and many fine relics of Mughal tombs and monuments.

Above Celebrating Holi, the spring festival, in New Delhi. People throw coloured powder and water at each other in fun.

Left A Bhil tribal woman at harvest-time.

The Jama Masjid mosque, Old Delhi This is a magnificent example of Mughal architecture.

The old city, a maze of winding narrow streets, alleyways and markets, has a more concentrated population of Muslims than any other part of the country.

Overleaf The splendid two and a half kilometre long Raj Path at dawn. The sun rises behind India Gate.

Delhi Twice a day the Jama Masjid is cleaned. A devotee makes a large duster by tying pieces of sheeting together and removes the fine sand dust which blows across from the sandstone Red Fort situated opposite.

Below A tribal girl from the west, proudly displaying her silver jewellery.

Living standards The contemporary middle-class Delhi-wallah enjoys one of the best living standards in the east. There are five-star hotels with expensive restaurants offering exotic oriental cuisine, shops and boutiques selling a wide variety of silverware, antiquities, gorgeous silks and softest Kashmiri woolens. Throughout the suburbs of the city, small enclaves of leafy residential colonies have been constructed, designed around communal gardens, each with their own shopping centres, schools, libraries and banks.

Right A Sikh gentleman and his son enjoy the spirit of Holi, the Hindu festival.

Left Kavita – a modern New Delhi beauty. An erstwhile television personality, she now works for an organization that promotes the sale of rural folk art and handicrafts. In a technological age where most city families have their own television set and refrigerator, conscientious groups of young people work to ensure that India retains her cultural heritage.

Index

Figures in *italics* refer to captions.

Series Editor: Alison Leach